# A TIME FOR EVERYTHING

Moving shadows gave birth to the measurement of time

# A TIME FOR EVERYTHING

*An Anthology of Verse and Prose on the Theme of Time*

Compiled by Reg Crang

*With illustrations by Michael Avery*

The Book Guild Ltd
Sussex, England

The Book Guild Ltd,
25 High Street,
Lewes, Sussex

First published 1998
© Reg Crang 1998

Set in Bembo
Typesetting by Raven Typesetters, Chester
Printed in Great Britain by
Bookcraft (Bath) Ltd, Avon

A catalogue record for this book is
available from the British Library

ISBN 1 85776 305 X

# ARRANGEMENT

# INTRODUCTION

Down the endless ages of the world's history man has been concerned with time in the short term – that is, with the moments and hours of each passing day. In the long ago it was simply a matter of judging how much light remained in the sky. But as civilisation developed and the devices for the measurement of time grew more sophisticated, we became ever more conscious of the progress of time throughout each day. Busy people are clockwatchers. In an active life our day's occupations are governed strictly by its hours and minutes. Working, eating, taking children to school or catching public transport are all occasions when we are slaves to the clock. Whether we are making it, killing it, playing for it or racing against it we are conscious of time for most of our waking hours.

Then as the years roll by and the pace of life slows we become more aware of time in the broader scale of our life span. We begin to wonder whether we are using our time on earth to the best advantage.

For most of us time is precious; we sigh for more hours in the day. But tedium can come suddenly, such as waiting for an urgent telephone call, or a long delay at an airport. For those unfortunates who are confined to hospital beds or eking out a lonely existence, time can lie heavily, a burden on the mind which cannot readily be set aside.

Time, in all its aspects, is such an important element in our lives that it has been the inspiration for some memorable poetry and prose. I hope that this anthology will give ready access to many of the more popular pieces and also introduce a few new ones.

# LIFE'S SPAN IN VERSE

---

*Let us begin with the oldest quotation in the English language on the sub-ject of Time, a biblical one from Ecclesiastes Chapter 3 verses 1–4:*

> To everything there is a season,
> and a time to every purpose under heaven:
> A time to be born, and a time to die,
> a time to plant, and a time to pluck out
> that which is planted;
> A time to kill, and a time to heal,
> a time to break down, and a time to build up;
> A time to weep, and a time to laugh;
> a time to mourn, and a time to dance.

*A time for joy is when a child is born into the family. The innocence of babyhood is recalled in this little poem by William Blake (1757–1827). The tenderness shown in this is in strong contrast with some of his other works such as 'Tyger, Tyger' and 'Jerusalem'.*

### Infant joy

> 'I have no name.
> I am but two days old'.
> What shall I call thee?
> 'I happy am
> Joy is my name.'
> Sweet joy befall thee.

1

Pretty joy!
Sweet joy but two days old,
Sweet joy I call thee;
Thou dost smile,
I sing the while,
Sweet joy befall thee!

*Perhaps the most familiar quotation on childhood is from St Paul's First Epistle to the Corinthians, Chapter 13 verses 11–13:*

When I was a child, I spake as a child, I understood as a child, I thought as a child: but when I became a man I put away childish things.

For now we see through a glass, darkly; but then face to face; now I know in part; but then shall I know even as also I am known.

And now abideth faith, hope, charity, these three; but the greatest of these is charity.

*Most of us regret the passing of our youth and early adulthood. I have chosen two poets who expressed their sentiments in this direction. The first is John Milton (1608–74) with an early poem entitled 'Time':*

### Time

How soon hath Time, that subtle thief of youth.
Stolen on his wing my three and twentieth year!
My hasting days fly on with full career,
But my late Spring no bud or blossom shew'th.

*Then this by A. E. Housman (1859–1936) from 'A Shropshire Lad':*

> Loveliest of trees, the cherry now
> Is hung with blossom on the bough,
> And stands about the woodland ride,
> Wearing white for Eastertide.
>
> Now of my three score years and ten,
> Twenty will not come again.
> And take from seventy Springs a score,
> It only leaves me fifty more.
>
> And since to look at things in bloom,
> Fifty Springs are little room,
> About the woodlands I will go
> To see the cherry hung with snow.

*Well, it is nice to know that Housman exceeded his expectation by seven years. But Time marches on and Robert Herrick (1591–1674) urges us to*

> Gather ye rosebuds while ye may,
> Old time is still a'flying.
> And this same flower that blooms today,
> Tomorrow will be dying.

*All too soon the popular song by Paul McCartney 'When I'm Sixty-Four' seems to have more personal relevance.*

## When I'm Sixty-Four

When I get older, losing my hair,
Many years from now.
Will you still be sending me a Valentine?
Birthday Greetings, bottle of wine?

3

*One person who saw the Grim Reaper approaching but was able to await him with quiet dignity was portrayed by Robert Burns (1759–96):*

## John Anderson

John Anderson my jo, John
When we were first acquent
Your locks were like the raven,
Your bonnie brow was brent;
But now your brow is bald, John
Your locks are like the snow;
But blessings on your frosty pow,
John Anderson my jo.

John Anderson my jo, John,
We clamb the hill thegither,
And mony a canty day, John,
We've had wi' ane anither;
Now we maun totter down, John,
But hand in hand we'll go,
And sleep thegither at the foot,
John Anderson my jo.

*(Note: A 'jo' is a Scottish sweetheart)*

*We have been looking at some of life's stages through the eyes of various poets but the whole span is neatly covered by William Shakespeare (1564–1616) in his famous 'Seven Ages of Man', from* As You Like It *Act 2, Scene 7:*

## The Seven Ages

All the world's a stage,
And all the men and women merely players:
They have their exits and their entrances;
And one man in his time plays many parts,
His acts being seven ages. At first the infant,
Mewling and puking in the nurse's arms.
And then the whining school-boy, with his satchel,
And shining morning face, creeping like snail
Unwillingly to school. And then the lover,
Sighing like furnace, with a woeful ballad
Made to his mistress' eyebrow. Then a soldier,
Full of strange oaths, bearded like the pard,
Jealous in honour, sudden and quick in quarrel,
Seeking the bubble reputation, even in the
Cannon's mouth. And then the justice,
In fair round belly with good capon lin'd,
With eyes severe, and beard of formal cut,
Full of wise saws and modern instances;
And so he plays his part. The sixth age shifts
Into the lean and slipper'd pantaloon.
With spectacles on nose and pouch on side,
His youthful hose well sav'd, a world too wide
For his shrunk shank; and his big manly voice,
Turning again toward childish treble, pipes
And whistles in his sound. Last scene of all
That ends this strange eventful history,
Is second childishness and mere oblivion,
Sans teeth, sans eyes, sans taste, sans everything.

'Six o'clock and all's well!'

# A MEDLEY OF TIME PIECES

*William Shakespeare figures prominently in this anthology simply because of the great volume of relevant material. Clearly he was obsessed by the relentless passage of Time. Again and again he reveals his dread of old age in phrases such as 'Time's fell hand' and 'this bloody tyrant, Time'. Perhaps he was aware that his own lifespan was destined to be too short for the complete fulfilment of his genius. We are fortunate in that he did not spare himself during his working life. His poetry and prose contain many vivid illustrations of the influence of Time on man and nature.*

*In this extract from 'The Passionate Pilgrim' – one of his only two long poems – Shakespeare draws a sharp contrast between youth and old age. The tone suggests that this was an early poem although the spectre of old age was even then in his mind's eye:*

> Crabbed age and youth cannot live together;
> Youth is full of pleasure, age is full of care;
> Youth like summer morn, age like winter weather;
> Youth like summer brave, age like winter bare.
> Youth is full of sport, age's breath is short,
>     Youth is nimble, age is lame;
> Youth is hot and bold, age is weak and cold;
> Youth is wild and age is tame.
> Age, I do abhor thee, youth I do adore thee;
>     O! my love, my love is young;
> Age, I do defy thee: O! sweet shepherd hie thee,
>     For me thinks thou stay'st too long.

*The sonnets abound with references to Time. In this one we may visualise an adoring swain, impatient at the way Time drags while awaiting his lady's return:*

## Sonnet LVII

Being your slave, what should I do but tend
Upon the hours and times of your desire?
I have no precious time at all to spend,
Nor services to do, till you require.
Nor dare I chide the world-without-end hour
Whilst I, my sovereign, watch the clock for you,
Nor think the bitterness of absence sour
When you have bid your servant once adieu;
Nor dare I question with my jealous thought
Where you may be, or your affairs suppose,
But, like a sad slave, stay and think of nought
Save, where you are how happy you make those!
So true a fool is love, that in your Will,
Though you do any thing, he thinks no ill.

*and Macbeth, on hearing of his wife's death:*

Tomorrow, and tomorrow, and tomorrow,
Creeps in this petty pace from day to day,
To the last syllable of recorded time;
And all our yesterdays have lighted fools
The way to dusty death. Out, out, brief candle!
Life's but a walking shadow, a poor player
That struts and frets his hour upon the stage,
And then is heard no more; it is a tale
Told by an idiot, full of sound and fury,
Signifying nothing.

*Then these memorable words, spoken by Richard II while held prisoner by Henry Bolingbroke, which reveal Shakespeare's mastery with a telling phrase:*

I have wasted time, and now doth time waste me.

*In complete contrast the next offering is my own firm favourite on the concept of Time. Regretfully it has to bear the label 'anon' as I do not recall its origin and a long search in every available work of reference has proved fruitless. I copied it on the back of an envelope long years ago from I know not where. To me it has a haunting beauty, its simple but expressive language giving a graphic description of how a timeless absence can be almost unendurable. I have given it the title:*

## Desolation

Slowly the seconds drip
into the minute bowl,
which overflows into the pool of hours.
Hours stream into days,
long days, until oceans of time
separates your love,
your deep abiding love
from mine.

*In our Norfolk village of Bramerton we lived opposite The Hall, a manor house which had been in the Blake family for a great number of generations. One day the Mr Blake of that time showed me his fine hunter watch, together with this charming poem – printed but anonymous – which had been composed for the original owner of the watch, a Mr John Blake:*

Could but our Tempers move as this machine,
    Not urged by Passion, nor delayed by Spleen;
But true to Nature's regulating Power,
    By virtuous Acts distinguish every Hour.

Then Health and Joy would follow as they ought,
    The Laws of Motion and the Laws of Thought;
Sweet Health to pass the present moments o'er
    And everlasting Joy when Time shall be no more.

'Oh dear! Oh dear! I shall be too late!' said the White Rabbit in *Alice's Adventures in Wonderland*.

*A. W. E. O'Shaughnessy (1844–81) in romantic mood:*

> We are the music makers.
> We are the dreamers of dreams ...
> For each age is a dream that is dying,
> Or one that is coming to birth.

*My lifelong favourite poet is Alfred, Lord Tennyson (1809–92). (Shakespeare, the supreme master of words, was on a plane of his own and cannot therefore be classified into any particular category of writer).*

*In Tennyson's long poem 'Ulysses', which is here abridged, the hero urges his fellow-mariners to make the most of time. He himself has an insatiable thirst for voyaging but knows that for him the sands of time are running out. Despite his stirring words, however, his crew take a different view when they discover an island paradise. That is the subject of another wonderful poem, 'The Lotus Eaters', the very antithesis of 'Ulysses'. Unfortunately it is not one which conforms to the theme of this book and so regretfully must be omitted, except for a few haunting lines which simply demand to be included:*

> There is sweet music here that softer falls
> Than petals from blown roses on the grass.
> Music that gentlier on the spirit lies,
> Than tir'd eyelids upon tir'd eyes.

*Well, that was from 'The Lotus Eaters'. And now this:*

## Ulysses

It little profits that an idle king
By this still hearth, among these barren crags
Matched with an aged wife, I mete and dole
Unequal laws unto a savage race
That hoard, and sleep, and feed, and know not me.

I cannot rest from travel. I will drink
Life to the lees: all times I have enjoyed
Greatly, have suffered greatly.
I am a part of all that I have met;
Yet all experience in an arch wherethro'
Gleams that untravell'd world, whose margin fades
For ever and ever when I move.
How dull it is to pause, to make an end,
To rust unburnish'd, not to shine in use!
As tho' to breathe were life. Life piled on life
Were all too little, and of one to me
Little remains: but every hour is saved
From that eternal silence.

There lies the port; the vessel puffs her sail.
There gloom the dark broad seas. My mariners,
Souls that have toil'd, wrought and thought with me
Free hearts, free foreheads – you and I are old;
Old age hath yet his honour and his toil;
Death closes all: but something ere the end,
Some work of noble note, may yet be done,
Not unbecoming men who strove with Gods.
The lights begin to twinkle from the rocks:
The long day wanes: the slow moon climbs: the deep
Moans round with many voices. Come, my friends,
'Tis not too late to seek a newer world.

Push off, and sitting well in order, smite
the sounding furrows; for my purpose holds
To sail beyond the sunset, and the baths
Of all the western stars until I die.
It may be that the gulfs will wash us down:
It may be we shall touch the Happy Isles,
And see the great Achilles, whom we knew.
Tho' much is taken, much abides; and tho'
We are not now that strength which in old days
Moved earth & heaven; that which we are, we are;
One equal temper of heroic hearts,
Made weak by time and fate, but strong in will
To strive, to seek, to find, and not to yield.

*To conclude this section of the anthology the choice falls on a short extract*
*from the funeral service for Diana, Princess of Wales at Westminster Abbey*
*on 6 September 1997 ... In an occasion which touched the hearts of a*
*nation, these moving words, of unknown origin, were spoken by Lady Jane*
*Fellowes, Diana's sister.*

Time is too slow for those who wait,
too swift for those who fear,
too long for those who grieve,
too short for those who rejoice,
but for those who love, time is eternity.

# TIME IN SONG AND VERSE

*There are numerous popular songs which revolve around the subject of Time. One which we used to sing in the 1930s had clever rhymes in the lyrics:*

## Time Was

Time was, when we had fun on the schoolyard swings;
When we exchanged graduation rings
One lovely yesterday.

Time was, when we wrote love letters in the sand,
Or lingered over our 'coffee and ...'
Dreaming the time away.

Picnics and hayrides and mid-winter sleigh-rides,
And never apart;
Hikes in the country and there's more than one tree
On which I've a place in your heart.

Darling, ev'ry tomorrow will be complete,
If all our moments are half as sweet,
Sweet as the time was then.

(Music by Miguel Prado, Words by S K Russell, 1936)

*Ah well, idealistic perhaps but a nice little story all the same. Regrettably, both rhyming lyrics and story-telling have fallen out of use in modern song-writing.*

*And now an extract from a Paul McCartney classic which allies rather wistful words to a lovely melody:*

### Yesterday

Yesterday,
All my troubles seemed to far away,
Now it looks as though they're here to stay
So I believe in yesterday.

*Time in the very long term is portrayed in these two verses from 'O God our help in ages past' (No.99 in* Hymns Ancient and Modern*).*

> A thousand ages in Thy sight
> Are like an evening gone;
> Short as the watch that ends the night
> Before the rising sun.
>
> Time like an ever-rolling stream
> Bears all its sons away;
> They fly forgotten as a dream
> Dies at the opening day.

*That presents us with a rather sobering thought. It will not do to dwell on it too long so let's cheer up with some comic verse from Lewis Carroll (1832–98):*

> 'The time has come' the Walrus said,
> 'To talk of many things:
> Of shoes, and ships, and sealing wax,
> Of cabbages and kings.
> And why the sea is boiling hot,
> And whether pigs have wings'.

*That first appeared in* Through the Looking Glass, *which also contained this little gem: 'The rule is, jam tomorrow and jam yesterday – but never jam today.'*

*Still with Lewis Carroll but this time from the incomparable* Alice in Wonderland *comes this parody of a much earlier and more serious poem written by Robert Southey (1774–1843) which appears on p. 56:*

'You are old, Father William,' the young man said,
    'And your hair has become very white;
And yet you incessantly stand on your head –
    Do you think at your age it is right?'

'In my youth,' Father William replied to his son,
    'I feared it might injure the brain;
But now that I'm perfectly sure I have none,
    Why, I do it again and again.'

*In the faraway days of charabanc excursions there was a popular song entitled 'There is a good time coming – but it's ever so far away!'. Despite the note of cynicism this was a happy song and had a cheerful influence; we sang it with gusto on homeward-bound journeys.*

# THE WORKS OF W. H. DAVIES

*W. H. Davies (1871–1940) has given us two very different examples of the way his time was spent. In the well-known short poem 'Leisure' he longs for more time in which to admire nature. In strong contrast 'The Lodging House Fire' gives a graphic description of the way in which his days were deliberately wasted.*

## Leisure

What is this life if, full of care,
We have no time to stand and stare.

No time to stand beneath the boughs
And stare as long as sheep or cows.

No time to see, when woods we pass,
Where squirrels hide their nuts in grass.

No time to see, in broad daylight,
Streams full of stars, like skies at night.

No time to turn at Beauty's glance,
And watch her feet, how they can dance.

No time to wait till her mouth can
Enrich that smile her eyes began.

A poor life this if, full of care,
We have no time to stand and stare.

*Davies' autobiography was published in two volumes, separated by a long interval. The first part, published in 1908 when he was only 38, is the very readable and amusing* Autobiography of a Supertramp. *By the time I acquired a copy in 1950 there had been 31 reprints.*

*Davies was a genuine hobo, not a professional author who adopts a mode of life in order to get material for a book. He left his native Wales as a young man and soon took up the life of a tramp, first in America and then in Canada. Over there the fraternity could live very well, trading on the good nature of generous housewives. Travelling in twos or threes they would exploit one town, and then make their way to the next on the railroad, riding either between or on the top of goods wagons. It was a dangerous business and a train-jumping accident led to Davies having a leg amputated. He returned to Wales but soon resumed his former life, selling bootlaces from door to door. Even on crutches he could cover many miles in a day. But poetry was in his blood and from time to time he would get a few verses printed on sheets of paper, hawking them round with his laces. By this means he could raise just enough to shelter from bad weather in cheap doss-houses. The next poem, resulting from his experiences there, illustrates the deadening effect on the mind when there is nothing to do but kill time:*

## The Lodging-House Fire

My birthday – yesterday,
Its hours were twenty-four;
Four hours I lived lukewarm,
And killed a score.

Eight bells and then I woke,
Came to our fire below;
Then sat four hours and watched
Its sullen glow.

Then out four hours I walked,
The lukewarm four I live;
And felt no other joy
Than air can give

Ten hours I give to sleep,
More than I need I know;
But I escape my mind
And that fire's glow.

O better in foul room
That's warm, make life away,
Than homeless out of doors,
Cold night and day.

Pile on the coke, make fire,
Rouse its death-dealing glow;
Men are borne dead away
Ere they can know.

I close my eyes and swear
It shall not wield its power;
No use, I wake to find
A murdered hour.

But all my day is waste,
I live a lukewarm four
And make a red coke fire
Poison the score.

*Davies eventually recovered his self-respect, married and lived comfortably on the proceeds of his autobiography. (Poetry never makes any money.) The second part of this work, entitled* Later Days, *has none of the appeal of the first volume.*

# SCIENTISTS ON TIME

*Although not strictly a scientist, H. G. Wells (1866–1946) made a name for himself in science fiction with* The Time Machine *published in 1895. This was about an invention which could supposedly transport its operator either backward or forward in time, in the manner later adopted by the BBC for the* Dr Who *series. In the book Wells makes an assertion that 'there is no difference between Time and any of the three dimensions of space except that our consciousness moves along it'. Later Professor Einstein also wrote of his conviction that Time was a dimension and it was incorporated into his famous 'General Theory of Relativity'.*

*In June 1996* The Times *published this report:*

### EINSTEIN PROVED RIGHT AS TIME FLIES

A Boeing 747 was transformed into a time machine in a rerun of a famous experiment made 25 years ago.

One of the most accurate clocks in the world was flown across the Atlantic and back. When it was compared with an identical clock in London on its return, the travelling clock had gained 40 nano-seconds (one nano-second is a billionth of a second).

The result demonstrates Einstein's general theory of relativity, which says that time can be gained or lost according to how fast a clock is moving, and whether it is moving in the same or opposite direction to the Earth's rotation. Gravity changes also affect time.

*Stephen Hawkings, in his popular book* A Brief History of Time *explains that a clock near the ground runs slower than one on high. But don't worry about it.*

## Ever Faster and Faster

Once upon a time there was just sunlight and darkness to mark the passing of time. In their simple world the early peoples of the earth accepted this natural arrangement and adapted their way of life to it. They were content, at least for a very long period of the world's history.

But after ageless aeons various ways were developed whereby their day could be divided into shorter periods. The shadow clock, which might be simply a small pole stuck into the ground, gave a rough indication of time as its shadow shortened in the morning sun and lengthened towards evening.

Then about 2000 BC the Egyptians devised the ingenious water clock: a regulated flow of water, either into a calibrated bowl, or out of one fitted with a carefully measured outflow pipe, marked the passage of time by the changing water level. Careful construction ensured that it was remarkably accurate. Another great advantage was that it did not depend on the sun's rays and so could operate both day and night.

A simple domestic measurement was obtained from the graded candle, with hourly markings spaced down its length. In the more sophisticated version of this, a metal tag was inserted at each marked space. As the candle burned down, the tag would tinkle as it dropped into the metal candle-holder, thus giving an audible warning, forerunner of the hourly bleep in a modern alarm watch.

Along came the more accurate hour-glass, whereby grains of sand slowly dropping from one measured bowl into another, recorded the passing of one hour. This of course gave rise to the expression 'the sands of time are running out'.

Specialised examples of this include the 3-minute egg-timer and the large 4-hour version, used for watchkeeping on some early ships. An example of this type may be seen in a Dorchester museum.

Civilisation developed further and ingenuity began to flourish. A giant leap forward came with the dialled mechanical clock, which would break the hour down into *minutes*. Splendid. What more could anyone want?

The pace of life quickens a little. Clocks are made to record *seconds*.

Things start to go faster. The second is split into tenths, then into hundredths. Still not good enough. *Milliseconds* are required.

Will the scientists never be satisfied? A millisecond is too long now. 'Much too coarse a measurement for our purposes' they cry. 'We need things called *nano-seconds*.' But I don't suppose it'll end there.

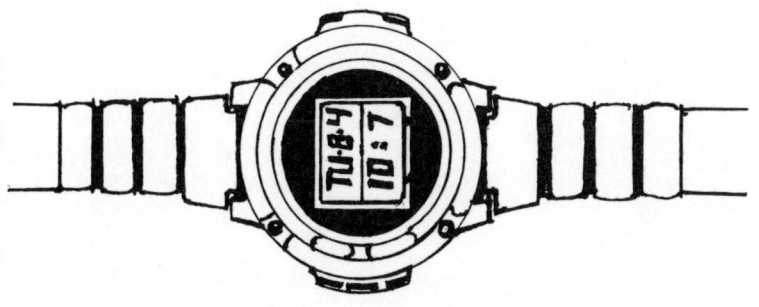

# TIME TO SYNCHRONISE

## 1. THE CALENDAR

In 45 BC Julius Caesar introduced a new calendar in order to bring a more accurate and uniform dating system into use throughout the Roman Empire. The Julian Calendar, as it was called, contained, however, a slight inaccuracy amounting to 9 minutes a year. Such a trifling flaw mattered hardly at all for the first few centuries but by 1582 the discrepancy had built up to ten whole days. Something had to be done. Because the religious calendar was the most seriously affected by the confusion over dates it was left to the church to rectify the matter. Pope Gregory XIII therefore issued a decree (known as the 'Gregorian Calendar') which removed the discrepancy and advanced the date by ten days. Most European countries complied but the change was not adopted by Britain until 170 more years had elapsed. (Britain was more Eurosceptic in those days.) This meant that by then the date would have to be advanced by 11 days in order to bring Britain into line with the rest of Europe and many other countries. The change was effected by a government order which stated that the day after 2 September 1752 would become 14 September. This aroused great dismay in the peasant classes who were afraid that their lives were being shortened! Riots broke out and many people marched through the streets shouting 'Give us back our eleven days!'

## 2. THE CLOCK

For well over a century after the calendar was standardised there remained an irritating discrepancy in clock times across Britain. Local time varied according to lines of longitude or in other words 'sun time'. Every town and village had its own time; people who owned timepieces set them by public clocks or perhaps the church bells. The variation amounted to about 30 minutes at the east-west extremities of the country. This did not matter much in the days when few people travelled far from their own district. But when Brunel's London to Bristol railway opened in the 1870s problems began to arise. The time difference of up to 11 minutes along the route brought great confusion. Railway timetables were printed according to 'London time' so that stations along the line needed a conversion factor to allow for the difference from local time. Missed trains became a frequent source of annoyance, particularly at the Bristol terminus. The London bound train from there left 11 minutes earlier than stated on the official timetable. So serious was this nuisance that the Bristol Corporation had an extra minute hand fitted to the public clock on the Corn Exchange. This then displayed both Bristol and London time simultaneously. That historic clock, since restored, may still be seen working today. Other clocks in Bristol soon began to show London time only, much to the annoyance of the local residents who had no intention of visiting the metropolis.

As public travel became more popular so the confusion over time variations increased. The Government decided to take action and in 1880 clocks across the country were standardised on Greenwich Mean Time.

Two-timer on the Bristol Corn Exchange

Anti-clockwise clock behind the bar of the Anchor Inn, Seaton, Dorset

# A TIME CAPSULE

*If Shakespeare had given titles to his sonnets he might well have called No. V 'Ode to a Pressed Flower'. To put it another way, it is a richly worded example of time crystallised:*

> Those hours that with gentle work did frame
> The lovely gaze where every eye doth dwell,
> Will play the tyrants to the very same
> And that unfair which fairly doth excel:
> For never-resting time leads summer on
> To hideous winter and confounds him there;
> Sap check'd with frost and lusty leaves quite gone,
> Beauty o'ersnow'd and bareness every where:
> Then, were not summer's distillation left,
> A liquid prisoner pent in walls of glass,
> Beauty's effect with beauty were bereft,
> Nor it, nor no remembrance what it was.
> > But flowers distill'd, though they with winter meet,
> > Leese but their show; their substance still lives sweet.

(Note: The word 'leese' would today be replaced by 'lose'.)

*A dried flower is a miniature time capsule, a relic of summer to admire on a winter's day. When making a long-distant visit to the Holy Land I bought as a souvenir a volume of pressed wild flowers, its covers made of polished wood. The ten specimens therein are as beautifully preserved today as when they were bound into book form nearly 60 years ago.*

# TEMPUS FUGIT

*This Latin inscription, so beloved of long-case clock-makers, is attributed to the Roman poet, Virgil, who lived from 70–19 BC. The full translation of the line from which the words are taken is: 'Time is flying – flying never to return.' This has been the lament of poets and others right down through the ages. In the vernacular it has been expressed as 'Enjoy yourself! It's later than you think!' For more eloquent phrasing we can turn to Andrew Marvell (1621–78), who was clearly impatient when he addressed this impassioned plea to the object of his desire:*

## To His Coy Mistress

Had we but World enough, and Time,
This coyness Lady were no crime.
We would sit down, and think which way
To walk, and pass our long Love's Day.
Thou by the *Indian Ganges'* side
Shouldst Rubies find: I by the tide
Of *Humber* would complain. I would
Love you ten years before the Flood:
And you should if you please refuse
Till the Conversion of the *Jews*.
My vegetable Love should grow
Vaster than Empires, and more slow.
An hundred years should go to praise
Thine eyes, and on thy forehead gaze.
Two hundred to adore each breast:
But thirty thousand to the rest.
An Age at least to every part,
And the last Age should show your Heart.
For Lady you deserve this State;
Nor would I love at lower rate.
       But at my back I always hear
Time's winged chariot hurrying near:
And yonder all before us lie
Deserts of vast Eternity . . .

Now therefore, while the youthful hue
Sits on thy skin like morning dew,
And while thy willing Soul transpires
At every pore with instant fires,
Now let us sport us while we may;
And now, like amorous birds of prey,
Rather at once out Time devour,
Than languish in his slow-chapt power.
Let us roll all our strength, and all
Our sweetness, up into one ball:
And tear our pleasures with rough strife,
Thorough the iron gates of Life.
Thus, though we cannot make our Sun
Stand still, yet we will make him run.

*Such eloquence surely deserved to win over his lady but we are left to wonder.*


*Some 500 years earlier the Persian poet Omar Khayyam had been reflecting on the same age-old concern. The manuscript of his famous 'Rubaiyat', which runs to well over a hundred verses, was however 'lost' for no less than 700 years. Then, in the middle of the nineteenth century, it was discovered in the Bodleian Library, Oxford. The scholar-poet Edward FitzGerald (1809–83) made two free and distinct translations of the work which did not, however, catch on with the public. In fact the first publication was a disaster and copies were 'remaindered' at a penny each. But when the poet Rossetti bought a copy he at once recognised its merit. He showed it to influential friends and together they ensured that the work received the acclaim it deserved.*

*One of my treasures is a boxed copy of the first translation, beautifully bound and illustrated. A used copy of the second translation cost a mere 10p.*

*Only a few verses can be reproduced here but they serve to illustrate how well the style and language of FitzGerald has been sustained throughout the poem:*

## THE RUBAIYAT OF OMAR KHAYYAM

1. Awake! for Morning in the Bowl of Night
   Has flung the Stone that puts the Stars to Flight:
   And Lo! the Hunter of the East has caught
   The Sultan's Turret in a Noose of Light.

7. Come, fill the Cup, and in the fire of Spring
   The Winter Garment of Repentance fling:
   The Bird of Time has but a little way
   To fly – and Lo! the Bird is on the Wing

11. Here with a Loaf of Bread beneath the Bough,
    A Flask of Wine, a Book of Verse – and Thou
    Beside me singing in the Wilderness –
    And Wilderness is Paradise enow.

16. Think, in this batter'd Caravanserai
    Whose Doorways are alternate Night and Day,
    How Sultan after Sultan with his Pomp
    Abode his Hour or two, and went his way.

18. I sometimes think that never blows so red
    The Rose as where some buried Caesar bled:
    That every Hyacinth the Garden wears
    Dropt in its Lap from some once lovely Head.

37. Ah, fill the Cup: – what boots it to repeat
    How time is slipping underneath our Feet:
    Unborn *tomorrow* and dead *yesterday*,
    Why fret about them if *today* be sweet!

51. The Moving Finger writes; and having writ,
    Moves on: nor all thy Piety nor Wit
        Shall lure it back to cancel half a Line,
    Nor all thy Tears wash out a word of it.

74. Ah, Moon of my Delight who knows't no wane,
    The Moon of Heaven is rising once again:
        How oft hereafter rising shall she look
    Through this same Garden after me – in vain!

75. And when Thyself with shining Foot shall pass
    Among the Guests Star-scatter'd on the Grass
        And in thy joyous Errand reach the Spot
    Where I made one-turn down an empty Glass!

*(Note: The first translation has only 75 verses whereas the second contains 110.)*

37

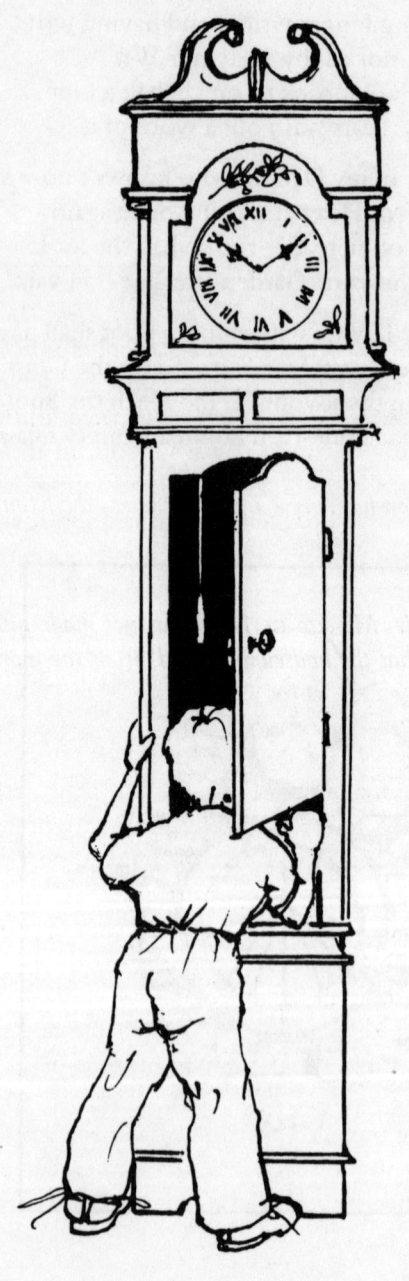

# TIME WARPS

There are many recorded examples of this phenomenon, some of them very convincing indeed. One which was related on television about 20 years ago concerned a housewife listening to an early morning news bulletin. In this she maintains that she heard brief details of a devastating earthquake which had just occurred. She asked a neighbour about it and also her husband when he came home for lunch. Neither knew anything of it. *The first announcement about the earthquake at Agadir, Morocco in 1960 was not made until 6 p.m. on the same day that the housewife 'heard' it on the morning news.*

Another instance that greatly impressed me and many others was the subject of a BBC television programme in which the central figure was a Captain Flowerdew, who lived near us in Bramerton, Norfolk. I came to know him quite well and he later consented to relate the story personally to a few of us who gathered in our home. He was an old man then, quiet and rather reserved, not at all the military type indicated by the title he still carried; one could imagine that he had risen from the ranks to the officer grade, perhaps in some branch of a non-combatant unit.

Although he had not travelled abroad he had been troubled for most of his life by vague recollections of an earlier existence, he knew not where. Even as a boy he used to worry his father by asking about it, especially when he saw sandstone cliffs, as there were at Cromer, where they often went on holiday. His father eventually forced him to drop the subject.

One day during his quiet retirement at Bramerton he was watching a travel programme which included some pictures of an ancient Middle East city. It was Petra, in Jordan, that 'Rose-red city, half as old as Time'.

As soon as he saw those pictures Captain Flowerdew jumped out of his chair in excitement. 'That's it!' he cried. 'That's the place! I know it! I lived there!' His wife thought that he had suddenly gone mad. She tried to calm him down, suggesting that he was seeing things. In a quiet old age herself she was not inclined to believe in any silly notions about a former life.

But over the succeeding days Captain Flowerdew was engrossed in recollections of an earlier existence, which in his mind went back to biblical times. He was convinced that he had met his death while defending Petra against invading Roman soldiers. What he did not know was that the city had changed hands several times and had then been abandoned during the twelfth century. Lying in a hidden valley it was 'lost' for over 600 years, probably buried under blown sand. It was not rediscovered until the nineteenth century, and being well-preserved it is now a sort of time-warp in itself.

Captain Flowerdew grew so confident in his story that others began to listen and it was published. Then it was taken up by the BBC, who were sufficiently impressed to make a television programme about it. They decided to put this remarkable story to an acid test, beginning by filming Captain Flowerdew in his garden at Bramerton. In front of the cameras there he drew a plan of Petra as he remembered it, a plan which was to be taken to the city by the BBC producer to compare it with the reality on the ground. A visit to Petra was arranged by the Jordanian Government, who were given permission to appoint a local television crew for the exercise.

During the course of the visit it was found that Captain Flowerdew had foretold with great accuracy what would be found in the city. Much of his information could never have been found in any book, with details of great diversity such as this:

1. Advice that the BBC truck being prepared was too wide to negotiate the narrow pass to Petra.
2. The source of the city's water supply. There was no sign of water when the team arrived but they dug down and discovered an underground spring.
3. The knowledge that a series of recesses in a cave wall, which had puzzled archaeologists for years, was used by soldiers to hold their name tags so that their captain knew who was on duty.

Many of Captain Flowerdew's other predictions also proved to be correct. The people who witnessed the events in Petra that day, including many journalists, were stunned by his revelations. He could not of course account for this phenomenon but to him the time warp of some 1,800 years was very real indeed.

# TIME REMEMBERED

Memory is linked directly with Time and hence has been the subject of much poetry which is relevant to our theme. First, some lines from my autograph book written by my future wife as I went away to the war:

> When Time who steals our cares away,
> Shall steal our pleasures too;
> The memory of the past shall stay,
> And all our joys renew

Algernon Swinburne (1873–1909) contributes:

> And time remembered is grief forgotten,
> And frosts are slain and flowers begotten.
> And in green underwood and cover,
> Blossom by blossom the spring begins.

## The Bard again: Sonnet XXX

When to the sessions of sweet silent thought
I summon up remembrance of things past,
I sigh the lack of many a thing I sought,
And with old woes new wail my dear time's waste:
Then can I drown an eye, unused to flow,
For precious friends hid in death's dateless night,

And weep afresh love's long since cancell'd woe,
And moan the expense of many a vanish'd sight:
Then can I grieve at grievances foregone,
And heavily from woe to woe tell o'er
The sad account of fore-bemoaned moan,
Which I new pay as if not paid before.
  But if the while I think on thee, dear friend,
  All losses are restored and sorrows end.

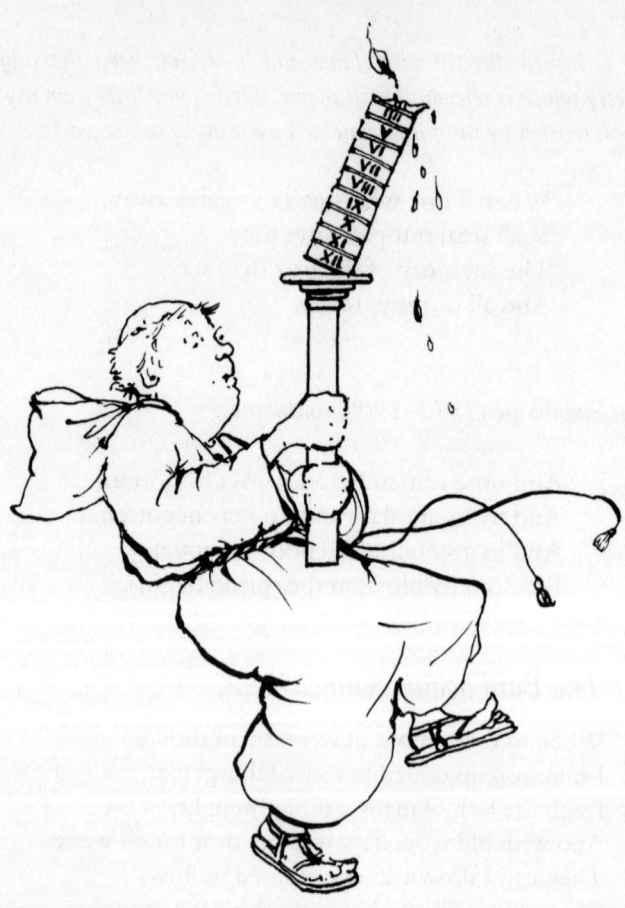

A graded candle clock

# TIME DEFIED

*Although from a physical standpoint Shakespeare appeared to dread the approach of old age, he remained confident that his work would endure. Frequently he would appear to shake his fist at Old Father Time, defying him to cause his words to be forgotten over the passing years. While this might be perceived as conceit, it is easy to forgive and no one doubts its truth. The sonnets contain many examples:*

## Sonnet XIX

Devouring Time, blunt thou the lion's paws,
And make the earth devour her own sweet brood;
Pluck the keen teeth from the fierce tiger's jaws,
And burn the long-lived phoenix in her blood;
Make glad and sorry seasons as thou fleet'st,
And do whate'er thou wilt, swift-footed Time,
To the wide world and all her fading sweets;
But I forbid thee one most heinous crime:
O, carve not with thy hours my fair love's brow,
Nor draw no lines there with thine antique pen:
Him in thy course untainted do allow
For beauty's pattern to succeeding men.
  Yet do thy worst, old Time: despite thy wrong,
  My love shall in my verse ever live young.

## Sonnet LX

Like as the waves make towards the pebbled shore,
So do the minutes hasten to their end;
Each changing place with that which goes before,
In sequent toil all forwards do contend.
Nativity, once in the main of light,
Crawls to maturity, wherewith being crown'd,
Crooked eclipses 'gainst his glory fight,
And Time that gave doth now his gift confound.
Time doth transfix the flourish set on youth
And delves the parallels in beauty's brow,
Feeds on the rarities of nature's truth,
And nothing stands but for his scythe to mow:
    And yet to times in hope my verse shall stand,
    Praising thy worth, despite his cruel hand.

*Time's defiance continues in two further sonnets:*

## Sonnet XV

When I consider every thing that grows
Holds in perfection but a little moment,
That this huge stage presenteth nought but shows
Whereon the stars in secret influence comment;
When I perceive that men as plants increase,
Cheer'd and checked even by the self-same sky,
Vaunt in their youthful sap, at height decrease,
And wear their brave state out of memory;
Then the conceit of this inconstant stay
Sets you most rich in youth before my sight,
Where wasteful Time debateth with Decay,
To change your day of youth to sullied night;
    And all in war with Time for love of you,
    As he takes from you, I engraft you new.

## Sonnet CXXIII

No, Time, though shalt not boast that I do change:
The pyramids built up with newer might
To me are nothing novel, nothing strange;
They are but dressings of a former sight,
Our dates are brief, and therefore we admire
What thou dost foist upon us that is old;
And rather make them born to our desire
Than think that we before have heard them told.
Thy registers and thee I both defy,
Not wondering at the present nor the past,
For thy records and what we see doth lie,
Made more or less by thy continual haste.
     This I do vow, and this shall ever be,
     I will be true, despite thy scythe and thee.

*Several sonnets addressed to a fair lady advocated a defence against the ravages of Time by ensuring that her beauty be preserved in offspring. Two examples:*

## Sonnet XII

When I do count the clock that tells the time,
And see the brave day sunk in hideous night;
When I behold the violet past prime,
And sable curls all silver'd o'er with white;
When lofty trees I see barren of leaves,
Which erst from heat did canopy the herd,
And summer's green all girded up with sheaves,
Borne on the bier with white and bristly beard,
Then of thy beauty do I question make,
That thou among the wastes of time must go,
Since sweets and beauties do themselves forsake
And die as fast as they see others grow;
     And nothing 'gainst Time's scythe can make defence
     Save breed, to brave him when he takes thee hence.

## Sonnet XVII

Who will believe my verse in time to come,
If it were fill'd with your most high deserts?
Though yet, heaven knows, it is but as a tomb
Which hides your life and shows not half your parts.
If I could write the beauty of your eyes
And in fresh numbers number all your graces,
The age to come would say 'This poet lies;
Such heavenly touches ne'er touched earthly faces.'
So should my papers, yellowed with their age,
Be scorn'd, like old men of less truth than tongue,
And your true rights be term'd a poet's rage
And stretched metre of an antique song:
    But were some child of yours alive that time,
    You should live twice, in it and in my rhyme.

*And now for another well-loved sonnet, arguably Shakespeare's best, and one in which the final couplet still maintains his belief in the immortality of his verse. Perhaps another reason for its popularity is the knowledge that English summers in the sixteenth century were just as fickle as those of today.*

### Sonnet XVIII

Shall I compare thee to a summer's day?
Thou art more lovely and more temperate:
Rough winds do shake the darling buds of May,
And summer's lease hath all too short a date:
Sometime too hot the eye of heaven shines,
And often is his gold complexion dimm'd;
And every fair from fair sometimes declines,
By chance or nature's changing course untrimm'd;
But thy eternal summer shall not fade,
Nor lose possession of that fair thou owest;
Nor shall death brag thou wanders't in his shade,
When in eternal lines to time thou grow'st:
    So long as men can breathe, or eyes can see,
    So long lives this, and this gives life to thee.

*(Note: In this context 'owest' means 'ownest'.)*

# TIME INEXORABLE

*In this final sonnet Shakespeare writes despairingly about the inevitability of Time's destructive power. No other poet shows the same depth of feeling about this aspect of time. Indeed Shakespeare often reveals a morbid fascination about what he regards as a destroying scourge which casts a blight upon beauty, whether it be in man, material or nature.*

## Sonnet LXV

Since brass, nor stone, nor earth, nor boundless sea,
But sad mortality o'ersways their power,
How with this rage shall beauty hold a plea
Whose action is no stronger than a flower?
O, how shall summer's honey breath hold out
Against the wreckful siege of battering days,
When rocks impregnable are not so stout,
Nor gates of steel so strong, but Time decays?
O fearful meditation! where alack,
Shall Time's best Jewel from Time's chest lie hid?
Or what strong hand can hold his swift foot back?
Or who his spoil of beauty can forbid?
    O, none, unless this miracle have might,
    That in black ink my love may still burn bright.

# TIME AS A CONSOLATION

*Although Shakespeare was so despondent about the passage of time, it is a comfort, when one is beginning to grow old, to know that not everyone looks on it with regret. Sometimes it can be a blessing, as when those who have lost loved ones are comforted by friends who say that time will lessen their grief. 'Time is a great healer', they are told. Disraeli is credited with the phrase 'Time is the great physician'.*

*W. B. Yeats (1865–1939) found consolation, albeit tinged with sadness in this:*

### When You Are Old

When you are old and gray and full of sleep,
And nodding by the fire, take down this book,
And slowly read, and dream of the soft look
Your eyes had once, and of their shadows deep;

How many loved your moments of glad grace,
And loved your beauty with love false or true;
But one man loved the pilgrim soul in you,
And loved the sorrows of your changing face.

And bending down beside the glowing bars
Murmur, a little sadly, how love fled
And paced upon the mountains overhead
And hid his face amid a crowd of stars.

*This consoling piece about the passage of time is the work of Robert Southey (1774–1843). Lewis Carroll's parody of it, which appears on page 15 is the better known, probably because it was written for the very popular* Alice in Wonderland. *The original was discovered, rather surprisingly, in the* Oxford Book of Children's Verse, *under the title 'The Old Man's Comforts and how He Gained Them'. This is an extract of four of the original six verses:*

'You are old, Father William,' the young man cried,
 'And pleasures with youth pass away;
And yet you lament not the days that are gone,
 Now tell me the reason, I pray.'

'In the days of my youth' Father William replied
 'I remembered that youth would not last.
I thought of the future, whatever I did,
 That I never might grieve for the past.'

'You are old, Father William,' the young man cried,
 'And life must be hastening away;
You are cheerful and love to converse upon death,
 Now tell me the reason, I pray.'

'I am cheerful, young man,' Father William replied,
 'Let the cause thy attention engage.
In the days of my youth I remembered my God,
 And He hath not forgotten my age.'

*On a day of bad news Macbeth consoled himself thus:*

> Come what come may,
> Time and the hour
> Run through the roughest day.

*Robert Browning (1812–89) actually savours the passage of time in this verse from. 'Rabbi ben Ezra':*

> Grow old along with me!
> The best is yet to be,
> The last of life, for which the first was made:
> Our times are in His hand
> Who saith 'A whole I planned,
> Youth shows but half: trust God, see all, nor be afraid!'

*George Borrow (1803–81) clearly enjoyed his time:*

> Youth will be served, every dog has his day,
> And mine has been a fine one.

*And finally, this delightful little piece from the pen of James Leigh Hunt (1784–1859):*

> Jenny kiss'd me when we met,
>     Jumping from the chair she sat in;
> Time, you thief, who loves to get
>     Sweets into your list, put that in!
>
> Say I'm weary, say I'm sad,
>     Say that health and wealth have miss'd me,
> Say I'm growing old, but add,
>     Jenny kissed me.

# TIME HONOURED

*This final section of the anthology pays homage to those who gave their time and their lives in the service of their country. Anyone who has been present when comrades were killed in action cannot help but think of the time lost to them when their young lives were cut short. The feeling is well expressed in these few lines which originated I believe during the Far East campaign in the Second World War:*

> When you go home
> Tell them of us and say
> For your tomorrow
> We gave our today.

*Laurence Binyon (1869–1943) wrote a few simple lines in honour of the dead of the First World War; they have been, and still will be, recited millions of times. In towns and cities throughout the country every meeting of the British Legion begins with these words:*

### For the Fallen (September, 1914)

> They shall not grow old
> As we that are left grow old.
> Age shall not weary them,
> Nor the years condemn.
> At the going down of the sun,
> And in the morning,
> We will remember them.

*Rupert Brooke (1887–1915) undoubtedly foresaw his own fate in two poems written in the year of his death. 'The Soldier' is very well known from its opening line:*

If I should die, think only this of me.

*I must however refrain from quoting the whole of this beautiful poem as it does not fall within the ambit of this work. The other is rather more appropriate and I hope that this one will provide a fitting end to the section and to this selection of writings on the eternal subject of Time.*

### The Dead

Blow out, you bugles, over the rich Dead!
　　There's none of these so lonely and poor of old
　　But, dying, has made us rarer gifts than gold.
These laid the world away; poured out the red
Sweet wine of youth: gave up the years to be
　　Of work and joy, and that unhoped serene,
　　That men call age; and those who would have been,
Their sons, they gave their immortality.

*I have been persuaded to add a small offering of my own. It does not presume to form part of the anthology; indeed it is entered as an addendum only because it begins and ends with the theme of Time.*

## Reflections on the Old Oak
## at Fingringhoe, Essex

Half a millennium standing here
on your chosen ground, seemingly immortal.

While dynasties of regal splendour
fade one by one into the mists of history,
your enduring presence remains,
in majesty surpassing all.

From one diminutive seed,
swelling into such a magnitude
that ten pairs of outstretched arms
could scarce encompass this titanic frame.

And yet . . .

Even one of Nature's mightiest creations,
that could o'ershade and shelter
five score men and yet leave room for more,
must still submit to human mastery.

For only man can wield the blade
to stay the course of wayward Nature;
restoring shape and form to such a symmetry that
eyes will still in wonder gaze
through countless ages more.

# ACKNOWLEDGMENTS

Grateful acknowledgment is made to the following for permission to reprint copyright material.

Jonathan Cape and the estate of W. H. Davies for 'Leisure' from the *Collected Poems of W. H. Davies* and for 'The Lodging House Fire' from the *Autobiography of a Super-Tramp* by W. H. Davies.

A. P. Watt Ltd. on behalf of Michael Yeats for 'When you are old' from the *Collected Poems of W. B. Yeats*.

The Society of Authors and Mrs Nicolete Gray on behalf of the Laurence Binyon Estate in respect of 'For the Fallen (September 1914)'.

The Society of Authors as the Literary Representative of the Estate of A. E. Housman for 'Loveliest of Trees'.

Anjana Ahuja and Times Newspapers Ltd. 1996 for the report 'Einstein proved right as time flies'.

The Publishers have made every effort to trace copyright holders of material reproduced within this compilation. If, however, they have inadvertently made any error they would be grateful for notification.

# INDEX OF AUTHORS

# INDEX OF FIRST LINES